SIMPLE PLEASURES

Entertaining

BLUE HERON BOOKS

Vancouver

First published in Canada in 2004 by
Blue Heron Books
9050 Shaughnessy Street
Vancouver, B.C. V6P 6E5
(604) 323-7100
www.raincoast.com

Adapted from the Simple Pleasures series first published in 1996 by Conari Press.

ISBN 1-897035-00-4

Printed in the United States
PC

11 10 09 08 07 06 05 04
 8 7 6 5 4 3 2 1

The paper used in this publication meets the minimum requirements of the American National Standard for Information Sciences—Permanence of Paper for Printed Library Materials Z39.48-1992 (R1997).

Simply Entertaining

I'm a big proponent of simplicity in all the domestic arts—simple food, simple crafts, simple gifts, and simple games for you and your family and friends. In this and all my books, I advocate getting back to basics—appreciating the smell of fresh-squeezed orange juice, the feel of clean sheets, sitting down with your whole family to enjoy a meal. Particularly when it comes to homemaking and entertaining, all of us, no matter how domestically challenged, spend a great deal of our lives on these routine tasks of life—cooking, cleaning, and the like. So we might as well get the maximum satisfaction from them. This is what I'm hoping *Simple Pleasures of Entertaining* will give you.

$\mathcal{M}$y husband is a rabid tomato-grower. After our enthu-siasm for freshly picked and eaten cherry tomatoes has waned and fall has arrived, then it's time for sun-dried tomatoes. Though I have actually dried tomatoes in the sun, a much more dependable and efficient method is to dry them in an oven for 5–8 hours, depending on the size of the fruit. After cleaning and splitting the tomatoes in half, I salt them lightly on oiled cookie pans and place them in a 170° oven. When they are dry but not crispy, I pack jars with the tomatoes and fill to the top with extra virgin olive oil (press with a spoon to make sure the air is all out and add more oil if needed to cover tomatoes completely). We have so many we give lots away, but I always save some for our-selves. In the middle of winter these make the quickest and sweetest tomato paste in the world.

5

This recipe never fails to get raves at parties large and small. It's simple, once you get the hang of the rolling-up process. I pound the chicken with a full wine bottle, but you can use a flat mallet instead.

6

4 skinless, boneless chicken breasts
waxed paper
4 ounces goat cheese
⅓ cup sun-dried tomatoes packed in oil, drained and
   chopped
2 tablespoons chopped fresh basil
2 tablespoons olive oil
⅓ cup chicken broth or white wine

Place the breasts one at a time between two sheets of waxed paper on a flat surface. Pound until ¼-inch thick. (You may go through several pieces of waxed paper.)

Spread 1 ounce of goat cheese on each chicken breast. Top each with 1 tablespoon sun-dried tomatoes and 1 teaspoon basil. (There will be some of each left over.) Roll up like a jellyroll and secure with toothpicks so that no filling is showing.

Heat the oil in a large skillet over medium flame and add the chicken, turning frequently until white inside and lightly browned on outside. Be sure the inside is thoroughly cooked; this takes 12–15 minutes. Remove and set aside on a warm plate. Cover with aluminum foil.

Add the broth or wine and the remaining sun-dried tomatoes and basil. Turn up heat to high and reduce liquid by half.

THE PARTY FAN

*C*reatively folded napkins add to the beauty of any place setting. Here's a folding method that takes no time at all. If you don't have napkin rings, use a bit of ribbon or raffia as a tie. First, fold the napkin in half to form a horizontal rectangle. Fold the rectangle into 1-inch accordion pleats, and put on the ring or ribbon. Then spread out the pleats at the top and bottom to create a fan.

8

*More than anything,
I must have flowers,
always, always.*
　　　—Claude Monet

PEACH OR NECTARINE CLAFOUTI

This is a marvelous low-fat dessert that's perfect for late summer when peaches and nectarines are abundant.

1 ¼ cups low-fat milk
¼ cup granulated sugar
3 eggs
1 tablespoon vanilla
⅛ teaspoon salt
⅔ cup all-purpose flour, sifted
1 ½ pounds peaches or nectarines,
   peeled, pitted, and sliced
1 tablespoon powdered sugar

Preheat oven to 350°. Grease a medium-sized baking dish. Combine the milk, granulated sugar, eggs, vanilla, salt, and flour in a mixing bowl; beat with an electric mixer until the mixture is frothy, about 3 minutes.

Pour enough of the batter into the prepared baking dish to make ¼-inch-deep layer. Bake for 2 minutes. Remove the dish from the oven. Spread the fruit in a layer over cooked batter and pour the remaining batter on top.

Bake until the clafouti is puffed and brown and a knife inserted in the center comes out clean, about 30–35 minutes. Sprinkle with powdered sugar just before serving. Serves 6.

Happiness depends, as Nature shows,
Less on exterior things than most suppose.
—William Cowper

Here's an easy way to decorate your backyard for a summertime evening get-together—or just for yourself.

> silk flowers
> one strand of small white
>   indoor-outdoor Christmas lights
> ½-inch-wide white or gold ribbon
> plastic or silk green leaves
> hot glue

Pull apart the silk flowers and discard the stem. Take the light strand and push a light through the center of one flower. Hot-glue the ribbon to one end and begin wrapping the strand of lights. As you wrap, hot-glue the leaf stem to the chord and cover the leaf stems with the ribbon.

Before you start, be sure to read the directions all the way through—making this does require some expertise. Above all, don't leave the little ones alone—the hot syrup can be dangerous!

1 ¼ cups sugar
¼ cup water
2 tablespoons rice wine vinegar
1 ½ teaspoons butter
1 teaspoon vanilla

In a medium saucepan over low heat, stir together the sugar, water, vinegar, and butter until sugar is dissolved. Turn heat up to medium and cook, without stirring, until the syrup reaches 265° on a candy thermometer. Pour onto a buttered platter (be careful not to be splattered by the hot syrup: hold the pouring edge away from you and pour slowly) and let cool until a dent can be made in it when pressed with a finger. Sprinkle the vanilla on top and gather the taffy into a ball. Take care in picking up the mass; it could still be very hot in the center.

When you can touch it, start pulling it with your hands to a length of about 18 inches. Then fold it back onto itself. Repeat this action until the taffy becomes a crystal ribbon. Then start twisting as well as folding and pulling. Pull until the ridges begin to hold their shape. Depending on your skill, the weather, and the cooking process, this can take between 5 and 20 minutes. Roll into long strips and cut into 1-inch pieces. Makes ½ pound.

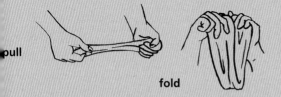

pull

fold

cut

CANDIED FLOWERS

These delectable treats are easy to create; use them on top of ice cream or cakes. Pick the flowers fresh in the early morning.

    violet blossoms
    rose petals
    1 or 2 egg whites, depending on how many flowers
     you use
    superfine sugar, to taste

Gently wash flowers and pat dry with a clean towel. Beat the egg whites in a small bowl. Pour the sugar into another bowl. Carefully dip the flowers into the egg whites, then roll in sugar, being sure to cover all sides. Set flowers on a cookie sheet and allow to dry in a warm place. Store in a flat container with waxed paper between layers. The flowers will last for several days.

Traditional wedding cookies are often served at other festive occasions as well.

½ cup powdered sugar
1 cup butter, softened
1 teaspoon vanilla
2 ¼ cups flour
¼ teaspoon salt
¾ cup chopped nuts, optional
    additional powdered sugar

Cream together the ½ cup sugar, butter, and vanilla in a large bowl. Sift in the flour and salt. Add the nuts, if using. Cover and chill the dough for 2 hours in the refrigerator or 10 minutes in the freezer. Preheat oven to 400°. Roll the dough into 1-inch balls and place on an ungreased cookie sheet. Bake until set, about 10 minutes. While still warm, roll the cookies in powdered sugar. Makes 4 dozen.

A BUNCH OF BEAUTY

*O*nce a week or so I buy flowers at the grocery store and take great pleasure in arranging that fresh bunch of flowers in a vase or two.

The other day at the store, one bunch of particularly vibrant dark pinks was much thicker than usual. I just had to buy it—pinching pennies can be so satisfying! Later I spent twenty minutes at my house happily making one arrangement after another, filling vase after vase. The florist had counted a few too many blooms into the rubber-banded bunch and had given me a bargain both satisfying and beautiful.

- Invest in a large beautiful vase—there's nothing like a heavy, well-designed, large, beautiful vase to display flowers and accent a room.

- Use odd numbers to create a pleasing arrangement.

FLOWER ARRANGING TIPS

SIMPLE PLEASURES

- Make an arrangement with "found" plants. This past Christmas my mother and I took a walk around our street. Someone had been trimming their evergreens and we ended up picking up several branches of different pines that were just lying in the snow. We took them home, she arranged them in a vase with a red bow and a few white mums, and we had an arrangement worthy of Martha Stewart.

21

- Think all one color of different kinds of flowers—all white flowers, or all red, or all pink. The variety of flowers and the monotone color really work together.

- The highest flower or green should be 2 1/2 times the height of the container, and the largest flowers should be at the bottom of an arrangement.

What love is to the heart, appetite is to the stomach. The stomach is the conductor that leads and livens up the great orchestra of our emotions.
—Gioacchino Rossini

This chicken is a low-fat entrée—provided you remove the skin when eating.

    4 chicken breast halves, with skin on
    salt and pepper to taste
    2 cups fresh raspberries and blueberries, mixed
    2 tablespoons chives, chopped
    1 onion, sliced

Rinse the chicken and pat dry. Create a pocket in each by loosening the skin with your fingers. Salt and pepper the chicken and set aside.

In a food processor or blender, purée 1 cup berries. Pour over the chicken, sprinkle the chives on top, cover, and refrigerate for several hours.

Preheat oven to 350° F. Remove the chicken from the marinade and place in a greased baking dish. Discard the marinade. In the pocket you have created in each breast, stuff ¼ cup berries and a quarter of the onion. Bake until the juices run clear when cut, about 45 minutes. Serves 4.

I love to have friends over for dinner but I don't have much time. And I'm not the best chef in the world either. But I accidentally hit upon a method for entertaining that solves all my problems. Over the years I have developed a few "guest menus"—for example, a delicious vegetarian stew for my non-meat-eating friends; that meal begins with a warm goat cheese, garlic, and sundried tomato appetizer that everyone loves and can be made in less than ten minutes. I've collected each "menu" in a notebook with lists of ingredients needed for each meal and a notation of whom I've served it to. When I'm having guests, I just whip out my notebook, see what I haven't served recently, and shop. Following are two of my favorite recipes.

WARM GOAT CHEESE APPETIZER

This is adapted from *Cucina Rustica* by Viana La Place and Evan Kleiman. It never fails to get raves—and requests for the recipe.

2 tablespoons olive oil
6 garlic cloves, peeled and sliced
8 ounces goat cheese
1 teaspoon dried oregano
5 sundried tomatoes in oil, drained and cut into slivers
2 teaspoons capers
pepper to taste

Heat the oil in a small skillet and sauté the garlic until golden brown. Set aside. Cut the goat cheese into ½-inch thick rounds and place in a single layer in a microwave-safe dish just large enough to hold the cheese. Sprinkle on oregano, tomatoes, capers, and reserved garlic. Grind pepper on top. Heat in the microwave for a minute or so until cheese is warm. Serve with crackers or baguettes. Serves 6.

These are fabulous—
and relatively low-fat.

PERSIAN LAMB KABOBS

1 pound lamb from leg or
   loin, trimmed of fat and
   cut into 1-inch cubes
4 tablespoons
   red wine vinegar
2 cloves garlic,
   chopped or pressed
1 teaspoon dried
   oregano

¼ teaspoon nutmeg
1 teaspoon cinnamon
6 skewers
1 green or red pepper,
   cut into chunks
1 large onion,
   cut into chunks
12 cherry tomatoes

Combine lamb with vinegar, garlic, oregano, nutmeg, and cinnamon.
Mix well, cover, and marinate in the refrigerator overnight.

Remove lamb from marinade and thread onto skewers, alternating with pepper, onion, and tomatoes. Brush meat with marinade and barbecue until lamb is medium rare, about 10 minutes, turning every few minutes. Serves 6.

*I'd rather have roses on my table
than diamonds on my neck.*
—Emma Goldman

This is a lovely item that will grace your table for months to come.

> tracing paper
> Scotch tape
> 2 15-by-19-inch pieces of washable fabric,
>   red or patterned with hearts
> thread to match
> straight pins

Tape two 8 ½-by-11-inch pieces of tracing paper together along the 8 ½-inch sides. Fold in half along the tape seam and cut out a heart. Unfold the paper, trace the heart onto the wrong side of the fabric pieces, and cut out the fabric.

Place the two hearts together, right side in, and pin together. Stitch along the outside of the heart, a quarter-inch from the edge, leaving an opening of about 2 inches. Clip along the curved edges and in the crevice. Turn right side out and slip stitch the opening. Makes 1 place mat.

I love to gather a group of people to make something best done in an assembly line—cookies or tamales, for example. I buy all the ingredients, invite over neighbors or friends, open a bottle of wine, and cook, cook, cook. The time speeds by, the work goes quickly, and everyone goes home with a big pile of whatever we've made that afternoon. As far as I am concerned, a cooking party is the perfect blend of conviviality and cuisine.

CONFETTI CORN CHOWDER

Here's a delicious chowder perfect for those cool, early fall evenings.

1 red pepper, diced
6 cups chicken broth
kernels from 8 ears of corn
1 russet potato, peeled and
  cubed
1 quart low-fat milk
1/4 pound bacon, fat trimmed,
  cut into 1/4-inch pieces

1 large onion, diced
1 medium zucchini, diced
salt and pepper to taste
5 tablespoons chopped fresh
  parsley
2 tablespoons chopped fresh dill
1/2 cup slivered fresh basil leaves

Blanch the bell pepper in boiling water for 1 minute. Drain and set aside.

Place chicken broth in large soup pot, and add half the corn and, the potato. Bring to a boil, reduce heat to medium, cover and cook until potatoes are tender, 10–15 minutes. Let cool slightly. Puree in batches, in a blender or processor, until just smooth. Transfer to a large bowl and stir in milk.

Saute bacon in the soup pot over low heat just until fat renders out, about 5 minutes. Add onion and cook until wilted, about 10 minutes. Add reserved puree, zucchini, and remaining corn kernels. Season with salt and pepper and cook for 5–8 minutes (do not boil.) Stir in blanched bell pepper and all herbs. Serves 6.

HEAVENLY HAM

This is a classic recipe that has graced many Easter, Thanksgiving, and Christmas tables. If you have managed to live this long without giving it a try, rectify the situation immediately (if you eat ham!). You're guaranteed to be delighted.

> 1 ham, about 5 pounds
> whole cloves
> brown sugar
> 1 20-ounce can pineapple slices in juice
> maraschino cherries

Preheat oven to 350°. Score the surface of ham with a knife and insert whole cloves in each intersection. Put in baking pan and bake. If ham is not precooked, allow 20 minutes per pound. If precooked, follow wrapper instructions. Pour juice from pineapple slices into a bowl. Add enough brown sugar to make a thin paste. Baste ham with glaze every 15 minutes or so. Cover the ham with the pineapple rings approximately half an hour before ham is done (use toothpicks to hold in place if necessary), and place a cherry in the center of each pineapple slice. Serves 8.

At the craft store, buy a set of clear Lucite napkin rings (the kind with an opening that allows you to put a piece of paper inside). Cut paper to fit inside the rings. Glue pressed flowers in any pleasing arrangement onto the paper, and cover the paper with clear, heavy tape, such as packing tape. Insert the paper into the rings. If you can't find Lucite napkin rings, you can glue pressed flowers directly onto wooden rings, then give them several coats of shellac.

CARAMEL APPLES

These make an incredibly wonderful barbeque treat at a Fourth of July party—one that all your friends must make for themselves! Be careful to let them cool completely before eating—caramel has a tendency to cool slowly.

> 4 medium apples
> small bowl melted butter
> small bowl brown sugar
> finely chopped peanuts (optional)

Place each apple on a shish-kebab skewer. Hold it over the coals, turning frequently, until the skin can be pulled off. Without removing it from the skewer, peel, dip apple in butter, then in brown sugar, covering completely. Hold skewer over grill and slowly turn until sugar becomes caramelized. Dip in peanuts if desired, and cool completely. Serves 4.

- Cut inexpensive white tissue paper into free-form ghost and goblin shapes, then use double-stick tape to display them in your windows. Have ghoulish faces peeking in from corners or silly ones popping up over the edges. You can even put these on mirrors in your house.

- Place dry ice in a large container with a bit of water to simulate a witches' brew. Be sure to keep out of reach of kids; it burns!

- Hang a string of lights with orange and black bulbs.

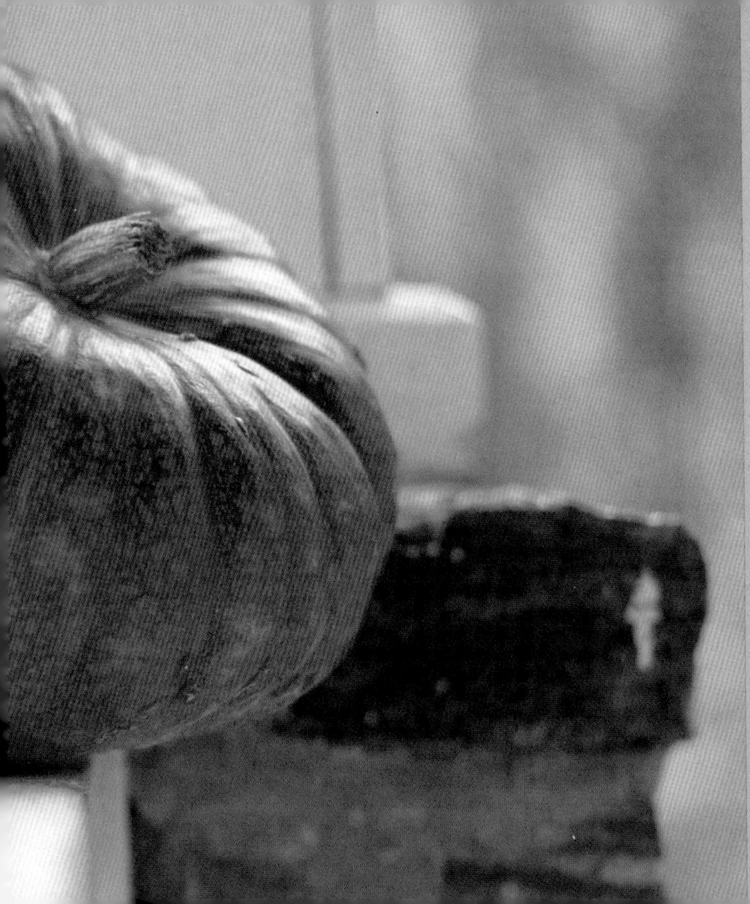

FRENCH ONION SOUP

What better way to get warm than with a wonderfully rich onion soup? Truly a simple pleasure.

1 pound large white onions
½ cup unsalted butter
1 cup dry white wine
7 cups beef stock

3 fresh thyme sprigs or ¼
  teaspoon dried thyme
Salt and freshly ground pepper
1 2-day-old baguette
2 cups shredded Swiss or
  Gruyere cheese

Cut the onions in half through the stem end, then again crosswise into thin slices. In a large saucepan over medium heat, melt the butter. Add the onions and wine and sauté, stirring frequently over medium heat, until onions are very soft and liquid is evaporated, about 15 minutes. Pour in the stock, add the thyme and salt and pepper to taste, and bring to a boil. Reduce heat to medium and simmer, stirring often until flavors are combined, about 15 minutes. Preheat the broiler. Cut the baguette into 6 slices. Ladle soup into 6 ovenproof bowls and place them on a wire rack or baking sheet. Place a bread slice on top of each bowl and top the slice with a liberal sprinkling of cheese. Broil 3 to 5 minutes, until cheese is melted and bubbly. Serve immediately. Serves 6.

THE DICTIONARY GAME

or people with a love of language and laughter, this is a hilarious game that can be played at home or in a car. All you need is a dictionary, pens, and pieces of paper. Here's how it works. Let's say you're "it". You pick a word that nobody in the game knows the meaning of. This is easier than you might think. Any dictionary is full of words that nobody has heard of. Words like "sirgang."

Once you've settled on a word, the game begins. You write out the exact dictionary definition, with all its variations, on a slip of paper. Don't show it to anyone. Meanwhile, everyone else writes down a made-up definition that sounds either deceptively legitimate or completely ridiculous—preferably both. The object is to imitate the dictionary style so well that you'll fool as many people as possible into believing yours is the real definition.

Once everybody has finished, they hand their paper to you, and you read out all the definitions, being careful to keep a straight face. This is easier said than done, because you'll end up reading definitions like sirgang: 1. carnivorous epiphyte native to Papua New Guinea; 2. premium sirloin; (sl.) a cut above; 3. green Asian bird; 4. gathering of hoodlums who have achieved knighthood; 5. long strip of serge, wrapped around the waist and knotted at the side; 6. insulated wire used in electronic circuitry.

Each person except you then tries to guess the real definition; that's where the point system comes in. You get two points if nobody guesses the real meaning of the word you chose, and everyone else gets one point for each person who chooses his or her definition. The game continues till everyone has had a chance to be "it," and the points are totaled. (The person who chose definition #3 for "sirgang" is well on the way to winning.)

CANDIED SWEET POTATOES

Many folks swear by this tried-and-true side dish.

1 cup dark corn syrup
½ cup firmly packed dark brown sugar
2 tablespoons corn oil margarine
12 medium sweet potatoes, cooked, peeled, and
  halved lengthwise
handful miniature marshmallows, optional

Preheat oven to 350°. In a small saucepan, heat corn syrup, brown sugar, and margarine to boiling; reduce heat and simmer 5 minutes. Pour ½ cup of the syrup into a 13-by-9-by-2-inch baking dish. Arrange potatoes, overlapping if necessary, in syrup. Top with remaining syrup. Add marshmallows if using. Bake, basting often, for 20 minutes, until well glazed. Makes 12 servings.

Perfection consists not in doing
extraordinary things, but in doing
ordinary things extraordinarily well.
—Angelique Arnauld

- Roll up your fabric napkins and tie with brown twine. Place a cinnamon stick or a leaf under the twine. Make a knot one inch from the end of the twine, and unravel the twine up to the knot.

48

- Gather enough pinecones to have one for each person eating with you. Use them as place cards by writing each person's name on a slip of paper and tucking it into the scales of the cones.

THANKSGIVING CENTERPIECE

*H*ere's an idea that is so simple you won't believe how good the end result will look. This Thanksgiving, why not decorate your tabletop with a collection of gourds and squashes? In the center of your arrangement, place the "Mayflower." To make it, find a large gourd in the shape of a boat and decorate with skewer masts and paper cutout sails. Finish off by scattering fall leaves, pinecones, and acorns among the squashes.

49

*H*ere's a tasty variation on the old Thanksgiving standby: cranberry sauce. It never fails to win raves when I make it. Don't be afraid of the jalapenos; it just gives it a zing.

SIMPLE PLEASURES

1 tablespoon vegetable oil
½ onion, diced
1 ½ tablespoons minced ginger
2 garlic cloves, minced
1 large jalapeno, minced
⅓ cup red wine
⅓ cup vinegar
1 cup brown sugar
1 teaspoon pepper

1 teaspoon cinnamon
½ teaspoon allspice, ground
cloves, ground coriander, and
ground nutmeg
½ teaspoon dried thyme
3 cups fresh cranberries
3 pears, peeled and diced
½ cup raisins
¼ cup maple syrup

In a large saucepan, heat the oil and add the onion, ginger, garlic, and jalapeno. Cook, stirring, over medium heat until onion is tender, about 5 minutes. Add the wine, vinegar, brown sugar, and spices, and simmer, stirring occasionally, until syrupy, about 20 minutes.

Add remaining ingredients and simmer until cranberries are cooked, about 10 minutes. Serve at room temperature. Serves 6.

- Say thanks. If you have trouble knowing what to say, you might want to pick up a copy of *A Grateful Heart: Daily Blessings for the Evening Meal from Buddha to The Beatles* by M.J. Ryan. Or hold hands and go around in a circle, saying one after another: "May the love that is in my heart pass from my hand to yours."
- Go around the table, with each person naming one thing they are particularly grateful for this year.
- Ask everyone to speak of who or what has been the greatest teacher in their life and why.
- Tell a story of how you celebrated Thanksgiving when you were a child.
- Invite the new person at the office who just relocated, or someone you know will be alone, to your home for Thanksgiving dinner and include him or her in your traditions.

I love baking pies: pumpkin, apple, blackberry. There's nothing that compares to a luscious fruit pie still warm from the oven and smothered with vanilla ice cream. That's my idea of heaven. Since my time is limited, I do cheat a bit and buy a frozen crust (Nancy's Deep Dish from Safeway is my favorite). But if you don't say anything, no one else has to know. Here's a recipe that has been a favorite of mine—and my guests—through the years.

¾ cup sugar
½ cup water
¼ cup red cinnamon candies (Red-Hots)
5 medium cooking apples (about 5 cups apple slices)
1 tablespoon flour
1 teaspoon lemon juice
1 tablespoon butter or margarine
9-inch double pie crust

Preheat oven to 400° F. In a medium saucepan, combine sugar, water, and cinnamon candies; cook until candies dissolve. Pare, core, and slice apples. Add to sugar mixture and simmer until apples are red. Drain; save syrup. Blend flour into cooled syrup and add lemon juice. Spread apples in a pastry-lined 9-inch pie plate and pour syrup over apples. Dot with butter. Cover with top crust, seal, and flute edges. Cut slits for escape of steam. Bake about 30 minutes until desired brownness. Makes 1 pie.

NATURAL BREATH FRESHENER

*P*ass around a bowl of mint sprigs after dinner to help everyone deal with the bad breath brought on by eating lots of garlic or onions.

*W*hen my in-laws are visiting, we sometimes prepare a late night snack (like ice cream with fruit sauce, or samosas with chai), change into pajamas, open the futon in the family room, bring plenty of extra blankets, spread out on sofas and mattresses, and either watch a scary movie or (my favorite) listen to the stories of my mother- and father-in-law. She tells great ghost stories and family stories; he relates tales of working for the Indian government. We stay up late, then fall asleep all together. It is then that I feel most like a part of their big, warm-hearted family.

SCENTED ORNAMENTS

Here's another wonderful and simple decorating idea. No, the ornaments are not edible!

1 4-ounce can ground cinnamon (about 1 cup)
1 tablespoon ground cloves
1 tablespoon ground nutmeg
¾ cup applesauce
2 tablespoons white glue
thread
glitter glue, fabric, or other decorating items, optional

In a medium bowl, combine cinnamon, cloves, and nutmeg. Add applesauce and glue; stir to combine. Work mixture with hands 2 to 3 minutes or until dough is smooth and ingredients are thoroughly mixed. Divide dough into 4 portions. Roll out each dough portion to ¼-inch thickness. Cut dough with cookie cutters. Using a toothpick, make small hole through the top of each ornament. Place cut-out ornaments on wire rack to dry. Allow several days to dry, turning ornaments over once a day. Create hangers by pushing a length of thread through the hole at the top of each one. Decorate as desired with glitter, beads, or fabric.

This is a bit different from mulled wine because it is served at room temperature. You must start at least 3 weeks in advance.

1 orange, peeled and sliced (keep the rind)
½ lemon, sliced
1 vanilla bean
6 whole cloves
1 750-ml bottle dry red wine
½ cup framboise eau-de-vie (clear raspberry brandy)
  or other brandy
6 tablespoons sugar

Combine sliced orange and lemon, orange rind, vanilla bean, and cloves in large glass jar. Pour wine over. Cover and place in cool dark area for 2 weeks.

Strain wine through several layers of cheesecloth into 4-cup measuring cup. Discard solids. Add framboise and sugar to wine; stir until sugar dissolves. Pour mixture into wine bottle or decorative bottle. Cork and place in cool dark area for at least 1 week. Can be made 6 weeks ahead. Store in cool dark area. Makes about 1 750-ml bottle.

CANDY CANE POTPOURRI

If you are a fan more of the scent than the taste of peppermint, consider this holiday potpourri.

4 cups dried peppermint leaves
3 cups dried pink rose petals and buds
1 cup dried hibiscus flowers
1 tablespoon whole cloves
1 tablespoon broken pieces of cinnamon sticks

2 tablespoons orris root (available at herbal stores and from catalogues)
20 drops rose essential oil
10 drops peppermint essential oil
1 tablespoon gum benzoin (available at herbal stores and from catalogues)

Combine all ingredients except gum benzoin and stir well. Add gum benzoin and stir well again. Makes 2 quarts.